101

Artefact E
has left f
touch. Pre
Sanctuary

sonal R
se who
the time, e
who was a
Royal West
was wounde
near Ypres in October 1917.

all towns
and villages, this one is at Dorking,
Surrey, and the cemeteries around
Ypres, such as Essex Farm Cemetery (see
opposite page), provide a rich source
of information. Used with local newspapers for 1914-18, the names on such
memorials can provide the starting
point for interesting investigations.

Photographic Evidence: those taken at the
time under study always provide a lot of
information in an interesting way. This
photograph shows soldiers by a derelict tank
at St.Julien, near Ypres, 1917. (photo:Daniel)

Above:some of the types of evidence used to help us understand the past.

The large square in the centre of the town of Ypres, West Flanders, Belgium. The square is called the Grote Markt or Grand Place, and is overlooked on all sides by fine buildings. The two most splendid buildings are the Cloth Hall, with its square belfry tower, and St. Martin's Cathedral with its tall spire.
(photo: Bill Caudwell)

   Ypres is a small market town lying on the flat land of the Flanders Plain in northern Belgium (see map on opposite page). The town has a long history. It rose to its greatest importance when it was a centre for the Flanders cloth trade in the Middle Ages. The Cloth Hall, where cloth was bought and sold, was built between the years 1260 and 1304. The Cathedral, which stands just behind the Cloth Hall across a small cobbled courtyard, was also built about this time. The remains of large defensive walls and ramparts around the town, still visible in part today, show how valuable a possession this rich cloth town must have been in the Middle Ages. Indeed, Ypres has a long history of sieges and occupations.

   The cloth trade died out several hundreds of years ago and today Ypres acts as a centre for the rich agricultural region around it. The colourful market which fills the Grote Markt on Saturdays reminds us of this. The beauty and long history of the town has also led to the development of quite a busy tourist trade. Several attractive cafés and small hotels overlook the Grote Markt.

   But appearances can be deceptive. A walk through the archway beneath the Cloth Hall belfry, for instance, reveals an obvious joining of newer building materials on top of a much older base. It soon becomes clear that there is a lot of newer material in the buildings and their interiors do not seem to match the style of the outsides. On buildings that look as though they should be several hundred years old dates such as 1926, 1932, etc. can be seen carved. The general appearance and 'feel' is of an old town, but the details tell us otherwise.

The whole of the town of Ypres is in fact an elaborate reconstruction.
The town we see around us today is not the Middle Ages 'original', but
was built between the 1920s and the 1960s.   The aim was to make it look
as much as possible like the old town, hence the realistic looking
exteriors and frontages but recent completion dates shown on some of the
buildings.   Something devastating must have happened here for all the
buildings, including the Cloth Hall and Cathedral, to have needed
complete reconstruction.   The magnitude of the destructive force which
must have reduced Ypres to rubble sometime in the recent past has
obviously been matched by an effort of equal proportions over the last
sixty years or so to restore it to its former appearance.   It was
in fact in the four years 1914 to 1918, a very brief moment in Ypres's
long history, that the town was completely destroyed. The destructive
force responsible for this was the guns of the German Army. Like so
many human beings, Ypres was a casualty of the First World War. So too
was the countryside around the town. It became a 'moonscape' of mud and
shell holes in those four years but today, like Ypres itself, destruction
has been replaced by green fields, reconstructed villages and peaceful
agricultural scenes, but some of that land is given over to the men who
came to Ypres between 1914 and 1918 never again to return to their homes.

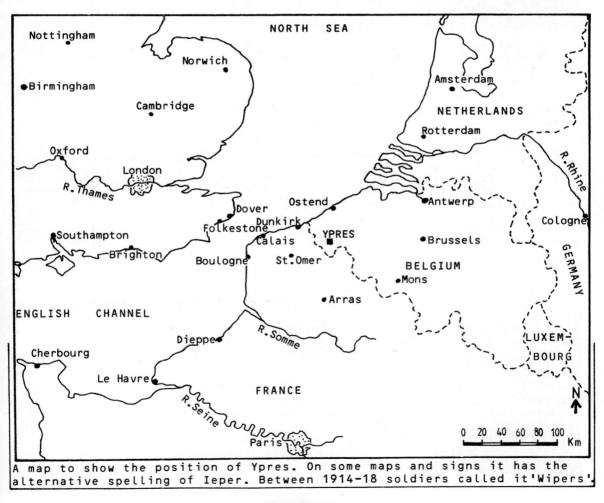

A map to show the position of Ypres. On some maps and signs it has the
alternative spelling of Ieper. Between 1914-18 soldiers called it 'Wipers'.

Ypres Before and After the War - Photographic Evidence:

as well as the artefact evidence of the reconstructed town, there is a photographic record of the destruction and reconstruction of Ypres. 'Photo Antony' and 'Photo Daniel' were two photographers who took pictures at the time the events took place in Ypres and some can still be bought, in postcard form, in the town today. They provide valuable evidence when attempting to explain what we see around us in Ypres today.

1912

Halles d'YPRES avant la Guerre
YPRES — The Cloth Hall, before the Great War

The first picture, opposite, shows us Ypres in 1912, i.e. before the war. The Cloth Hall and the Cathedral are thus the original 13th. and 14th. century buildings. Note the virtual absence of cars and also the stubby 'spire' on top of the Cathedral. The scene is one of peace, with time and space to stroll in the cobbled square.

The other pictures on this page show a very different scene. The one on the right (Antony) and the one below (Daniel) show what was left of Ypres in 1918 after the war. The stump of the Cloth Hall belfry and the

1918

1918

skeleton of the once lovely Cathedral are the only remnants of any significance to stand out from the rubble of Ypres after four years of heavy bombardment by German shells. As can be seen from the picture on the left, there was virtually nothing of the houses left standing at all. It was a barren waste as far as the eye could see.

3

The picture seen opposite (Daniel) was taken in the 1920's or 30's (the design of the cars helps date it). It shows the Cloth Hall half rebuilt and the footings of the rest laid out. The already completely re-built Cathedral is seen as we can never see it today now that the completed Cloth Hall blocks this view from the Grote Markt. Take a good look at the Cathedral

spire. It is now as it was intended in the original plans for the building - a fine topping to a splendid building. So, in that detail Ypres is better off than before 1914. In some other ways it is not. Note the way in which the number of cars is gradually increasing until in the final picture below (Daniel), taken in the 1960's, the centre of the Grote Markt has become more of a car park than a peaceful place to walk. However, Ypres has risen from the rubble and we can only wonder at the effort which achieved this in such relatively short time. By comparing the photographs for 1912 and the 1960's we can see how well the task of reconstruction was done and how faithfully reproduced, externally at least, the buildings have been. This is especially true of the Cloth Hall and Cathedral for which detailed plans, and, as we have seen, photographs existed which made rebuilding easier. All this work was paid for by

Germany as one of the penalties imposed upon her by the Treaty of Versailles which officially ended the war in 1919. This was but one of the 'costs' Germany had to pay for losing the war, the other and more tragic one being the loss of so many of her young men in the fighting. Both sides suffered almost equally in this respect. It is difficult, there-fore, to speak of 'winners'and 'losers'.

The bombardment of Ypres started on Nov.22nd.1914 once the German army found that the town stood in the way of its westwards march into France. This picture shows the ruins of the Grote Markt in Ypres with a group of Australian soldiers passing the shattered Cloth Hall on their way up to the front on 25th.Oct.1917. The soldiers in the background are moving in a direction away from the front line, but no-one was safe even when in Ypres itself as it was persistently shelled by German guns ranged in a close semi-circle round the town. (IWM E4612)

Having discovered what Ypres was like before and after the war, the task now was to find evidence of what Ypres was like during the war itself. Fortunately, there is an excellent museum in Ypres with maps, photographs, models, and many artefacts that help the visitor re-live Ypres's most desperate years. The museum is in the reconstructed Cloth Hall itself, in fact on the ground floor just about where the lorries are parked amongst the ruins of the Hall seen in the photograph above. Many pictures like that above and on the opposite page can be seen in the museum and provide detailed evidence of the past. However, the photographs shown on these two pages, and elsewhere in the booklet, come from an important source of such evidence nearer to home than Ypres i.e. the Photographic Department of the Imperial War Museum in London. Photographs can be studied there, under the watchful eye of helpful staff, and copies ordered. It is important to contact the Museum first in order to arrange a visit and give an idea of what it is that you wish to study because they have thousands of photographs! (for their address see the back cover). The Museum is obviously worth visiting for the marvellous exhibits too.

As well as photographs of Ypres taken between 1914 and 1918, we also have the memories of those who fought in the war to help bring alive

The bombardment of Ypres continued and the town was even further destroyed as this picture, taken in Sept.1918, shows. Gunner Stokes (see below) was lucky to get through Ypres safely as it was always possible to be hit by a shell as the wrecked ammunition limber in this picture has been.   (IWM Q11759)

those dreadful years. First-hand oral accounts are an important source of evidence in the study of people and events in the past. See, for example, the section in this booklet devoted to Frank Bastable's memories. For her book 'They Called it Passchendaele' Lyn Macdonald collected many such memories and used them to reconstruct what life was like for the ordinary soldier in the bitter fight for the Passchendaele Ridge near Ypres in 1917. Lyn Macdonald has been kind enough to allow the use of some of this very important evidence of the past in this booklet. Her book represents an excellent example of this approach to historical study and could be used as such, as well as to find out more about the battles that took place around Ypres in 1917. One of the contributors to her study, Gunner B.O.Stokes 13th.Bty.New Zealand Field Artillery, describes Ypres as he saw it when he passed through it on Oct.3rd.1917 while taking shells up to the front line:

> We passed through Ypres, my first time in the town. It
> is a pitiable sight now, shell-shattered and in ruins,
> with the famous Cloth Hall looking stark and naked with
> one wall standing. The traffic on the road was very
> heavy. As I passed through for the first time I marvelled
> and wondered at the immensity of war and the sad state
> of Ypres.

The Menin Gate, Ypres, seen here flanked by the remnants of the old town walls. The town lies inside the walls to the left, while the road to Menin, and the front line in 1914-18, leads off to the right.
(photo:Ern.Thill,Brussels)

One impressive building in Ypres that is not a reconstruction is the Menin Gate. As the inscription states it is a memorial to the armies of the British Empire who defended Ypres between 1914 and 1918, and to those who fell but have no known graves, so it was obviously built after the war. In fact, it was completed in 1927 and pictures taken at the time show large crowds of ex-servicemen and families of the fallen watching the dedication ceremony. The Menin Gate poses two questions to us today:why build a gate on this spot to commemorate and record the names of those who fell in the battles around Ypres?;and why did so many who fell have no known graves?.

All the evidence so far has suggested that Ypres,though destroyed by the Germans was not occupied by them. This is true,they were close enough to shell the town, but to encounter them at first hand the Allied soldiers marched out of Ypres the short distance 'up' to the front line where the two armies met in a prolonged stalemate. One of the main routes to the front line east of Ypres was along the Menin road, not that it was always recognisable as a road. Constant bombardment had reduced it to a smudge in the landscape of mud and shellholes. It was because it was the 'gateway' to the front line that this spot was chosen

for the site of the magnificent memorial gate we see today. Two lions flanked the pre-war 'gate'. Today one lion proudly tops the memorial gate staring, head erect, eastwards towards the old front line. Australia has the original lions as a memorial to her many men who died at Ypres.

Looking through the Menin Gate, the Cloth Hall belfry is clearly visible. The purpose of the Gate is shown by the inscription.
(photo:"Cypra",Ypres)

The Menin 'gate', Sept.20th.1917, with the shattered Cloth Hall belfry barely visible through the dust raised by the troops and transports on their way up to the front along the Menin road. The 'gate' is no more than a gap in the town's old walls which can be seen beyond the mounted soldiers.   (IWM E1394)

We turn once again to contemporary photographic evidence for knowledge of what the Menin 'gate' looked like during the 1914-18 war. The Imperial War Museum picture above shows that it was no more than a break in the town walls through which men, horses, guns and lorries passed as quickly as possible. It would have been an obvious target for German artillery. Any cover which the ruined town of Ypres offered was lost once you were outside of the town to the east. Another of the men who recounted his experiences of the war to Lyn Macdonald, Cpl.J.Pincombe of the 1st.Btn.Queen's Westminster Rifles gives us a personal account of what the Menin road, the route to the front, was like in 1917:

> We had to go through Ypres and up the Menin Road, because the battalion was in Glencorse Wood. The Menin Road was the artery of the battlefield. It was an extraordinary panorama, half frightening, half exciting. Everywhere, as far as you could see, there were spurts of earth from shells bursting and bursts of shrapnel and high explosives and men looking like ants in the distance. But as we got nearer we could see that they were stretcher-bearers coming through the mud to bring the wounded out. They were up to their knees in it, wallowing in it, struggling up carrying their stretchers to the field dressing stations at the roadside. ...As far as you could see in front of you and to either side, there was nothing but mud, mud, mud for miles and just a few stumps of trees here and there and all hell let loose all round you.

The notorious Menin Road, looking directly eastwards to the front line, Sept.27th.1917. 'Hellfire Corner' seen signed here, about 1½km. from Ypres, was a particularly dangerous place because German guns were always trained on it and, despite the canvas screens used to hide movement, were almost always sure of hitting something because it was such a busy spot. The Germans came this close to Ypres in 1918. (IWM E1889)

Cpl.J.Pincombe continues:

> Just as we passed Hellfire Corner we came on a young chap. Just about eighteen I should think. He was staggering all over the road. Didn't know where he was, didn't know what he was doing, just walking back.... .

You will have noticed that the previous two pages, and this one, have used a 'then and now' method of historical study.This is where photographs taken at the time of an event are compared with modern pictures of the same spot,e.g. Hellfire Corner'then and now' shown on this page. This approach to historical study has been most effectively and interestingly employed by John Giles in his book 'The Ypres Salient:Flanders Then and Now'. Anyone who is interested in finding out more about Ypres, or in using this approach in any study of their own,no matter what topic, could make good use of this book.

'Hellfire Corner' today, this time looking west into Ypres with the Cathedral spire visible in the distance.

Getting the wounded back through the sea of mud and water-filled shell holes. These were the conditions at the battle front near Ypres in which as many men died by drowning as by the direct effect of the shell or bullet. This stretcher party at least has the benefit of a duck-board track, but more often than not they had to struggle knee-deep through the mud. Photograph taken 15th.Feb.1918.   (IWM Q10661)

The other question that the Menin Gate we see today posed was why so many of those who died in the battles around Ypres have no known graves? There are the names of 54,896 such men from Britain, Canada, New Zealand, Australia, South Africa, India and other nations of the then British Empire carved on the walls of the Gate. An inscription reads: 'Here are recorded the names of officers and men who fell in Ypres Salient but to whom the fortunes of war denied the known and honoured burial given to their comrades in death'. What must conditions have been like to lead to this?. The photograph above helps answer this question for us. So too does a personal account of what it was like, again given to Lyn Macdonald, by Pte.G.Giggins, 62 Machine Gun Company:

Well, the front-line dead - a lot of people won't like this-they're simply dead. You can't do much about them. In most of the attacks, if they were killed they just had to lie there until they disappeared under the mud. That was the reason we had so many missing. When a fellow gets hit by a splinter or shell, or even a bullet, he collapses at the knees and usually falls face forward because of the weight on his back, which means you've only got to have a few inches of mud and he drowns in the mud. ..The thing was that you couldn't do anything for the dead. ..The most important thing is to get the wounded back because they do stand a chance.

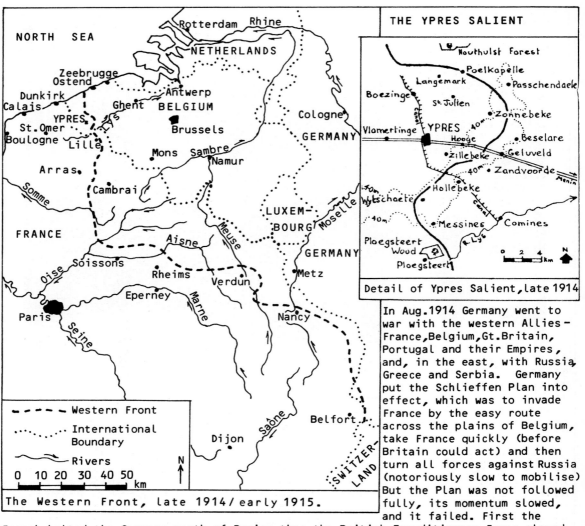

Detail of Ypres Salient, late 1914

The Western Front, late 1914/ early 1915.

Legend:
- – – – Western Front
- · · · · · International Boundary
- ∿∿∿ Rivers
- 0 10 20 30 40 50 km
- N

In Aug.1914 Germany went to war with the western Allies – France, Belgium, Gt.Britain, Portugal and their Empires, and, in the east, with Russia, Greece and Serbia. Germany put the Schlieffen Plan into effect, which was to invade France by the easy route across the plains of Belgium, take France quickly (before Britain could act) and then turn all forces against Russia (notoriously slow to mobilise) But the Plan was not followed fully, its momentum slowed, and it failed. First the French halted the Germans north of Paris; then the British Expeditionary Force slowed them at Mons; fighting took place on the Aisne to which the Germans had retreated; and then the Germans had to spread their forces to the north and south to avoid being out-flanked. The result was that the two sides now faced each other dug into parallel lines of trenches, called the Western Front, running from the Swiss border to the North Sea coast. The failure of the Plan gave Britain a chance to get more troops over to France. To prevent this the Germans attacked in the Ypres area in an attempt to reach and take the Channel ports of Calais and Boulogne. It thus became vital for the British to hold Ypres in order to prevent this from happening. They did so for four years, in which hundreds died on 'normal' days and thousands in the 'Battles of Ypres'.

The British front line at Ypres projected into German-held territory. Such a 'bulge in a line of trenches' is known as a 'salient'. Men defending such a line are laid open to attack on three sides at once, which is why the Ypres Salient was hated by the British and Empire soldiers who defended it 1914-18. It was made worse by the fact that the Germans held the semi-circle of low ridges to the east and south of Ypres for much of that time which allowed them to see, and shoot at, anything that moved. The ridges were taken, lost, and retaken in those four years, but Ypres, and the Channel ports, were never taken by the Germans.

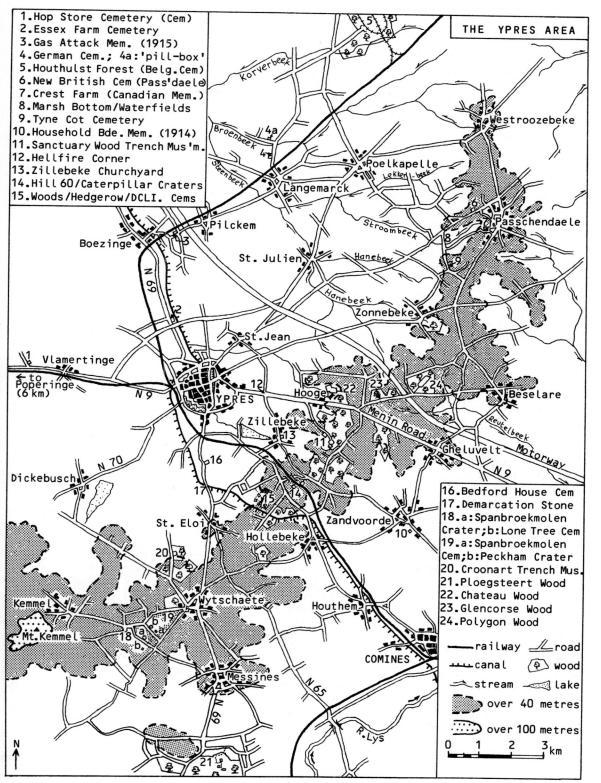

THE YPRES AREA

1. Hop Store Cemetery (Cem)
2. Essex Farm Cemetery
3. Gas Attack Mem. (1915)
4. German Cem.; 4a:'pill-box'
5. Houthulst Forest (Belg.Cem)
6. New British Cem (Pass'daele)
7. Crest Farm (Canadian Mem.)
8. Marsh Bottom/Waterfields
9. Tyne Cot Cemetery
10. Household Bde. Mem. (1914)
11. Sanctuary Wood Trench Mus'm.
12. Hellfire Corner
13. Zillebeke Churchyard
14. Hill 60/Caterpillar Craters
15. Woods/Hedgerow/DCLI. Cems

16. Bedford House Cem
17. Demarcation Stone
18. a:Spanbroekmolen
Crater;b:Lone Tree Cem
19. a:Spanbroekmolen
Cem;b:Peckham Crater
20. Croonart Trench Mus.
21. Ploegsteert Wood
22. Chateau Wood
23. Glencorse Wood
24. Polygon Wood

railway   road
canal   wood
stream   lake
over 40 metres
over 100 metres

0   1   2   3 km

Westroozebeke
Poelkapelle
Langemarck
Passchendaele
Pilckem
Boezinge
St. Julien
Zonnebeke
St. Jean
Vlamertinge
to Poperinge (6 km)
YPRES
Hooge
Beselare
Zillebeke
Gheluvelt
Menin Road Motorway
Dickebusch
Zandvoorde
St. Eloi
Hollebeke
Houthem
Kemmel
Mt. Kemmel
Wytschaete
COMINES
Messines

Korverbeek
Broenbeek
Steenbeek
Lekker beek
Stroombeek
Hanebeek
Hanebeek
Reutelbeek
R.Lys

N 69
N 9
N 70
N 65

12

THE BATTLES AROUND YPRES 1914-1918:

FIRST YPRES,1914: the first battle of Ypres began in Oct. and lasted into Nov.1914. Fierce fighting took place throughout the Salient, the Allied troops being far outnumbered by the German forces. The loss of the Messines Ridge in the southern sector was a severe blow as it meant that the Germans could overlook Ypres and the land before it from this higher ground. Defence of the Menin Road was especially fierce, and by holding the Ridge around Hooge and taking part of the higher ground near Zonnebeke, the Salient was held and Ypres saved. In the process of halting the German army's march into France, both sides lost the majority of their pre-war regular soldiers.

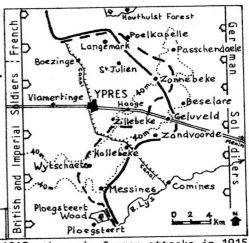

First Battle of Ypres 1914
——— front line 22,Oct.'14
-·-·- front line 22,Nov.'14

SECOND YPRES,1915: the main German attacks in 1915 were concentrated in the central and northern sectors of the Salient, from Hill 60 to Langemarck. The Germans were prepared to try anything to get a breakthrough. On Apr.22nd.1915 they released poisonous gas as part of an attack, for the first time on the Western Front, in the Langemarck and Pilckem area and made a major advance towards Ypres as a result. Eventually the whole of the Passchendaele Ridge, the St.Julian area, Hooge, and Hill 60 fell to the Germans. The Salient was now much smaller than in 1914 and Ypres was being threatened by German forces now in possession of the encircling Passchendaele and Messines Ridges.

Second Battle of Ypres 1915; - Gas!
——— front line 21.Apr. ⇧ gas.
- - - German advance after gas attack of 22.Apr.'15.
·····– final line May 1915.

THE BATTLE OF MESSINES,June 1917: so far the story had been one of German attacks and Allied defence. 1917 was to be the year of Allied attacks against the Germans in the Ypres area. The aim of the planned Allied offensive was to break out of the Ypres Salient by pushing eastwards across Flanders and possibly linking up with a British sea-born invasion of the German occupied Belgian coast. The first objective in this plan was to remove the Germans from their vantage point on the Messines Ridge. Beginning in 1915 and continuing into early 1917, tunnellers were at work digging under the German positions on the Ridge and laying high - explosive mines from Hill 60 in the north to near Ploegsteert Wood in the south. A great deal of fighting took place during this time, both above and below ground, to prevent the Germans discovering the tunnels and mines. At 3.10 a.m. on the morning of June 7th,1917 nineteen huge mines were all exploded at the same moment along the Ridge. An immediate attack followed the explosions and the Ridge was taken.

Battle of Messines, June 1917
——— front line 7,Jun.'17.
- - - front line 15,Jun.'17.
▰▰ the taking of the Messines Ridge.

THIRD YPRES, July–Nov. 1917: the next stage in the Allied offensive was to recapture the central and northern sectors of the Salient, particularly the Passchendaele Ridge. This was to prove much more difficult than Messines. A number of smaller ridges had to be taken before the main Ridge was even reached. A 3km. advance was enough to take the Messines Ridge, but it was about 8km. to the foot of the Passchendaele Ridge and the Germans defended every inch of the way!. This is why 'Third Ypres'was actually a number of battles lasting nearly three and a half months. What made the situation even worse was the mud and water through which the soldiers had to try to move forward. Constant rain through the summer turned the Flanders clay into a quagmire. The bombardment by our own heavy guns contributed to this by destroying field drains and stream banks. Men were as likely to drown in this mud as get killed by a bullet or shell, either way thousands of men disappeared into the mud never to be seen again. Even horses and big guns went in too. It was sheer hell; 150,000 Allied soldiers died in the fourteen week campaign. The final phase of Third Ypres, the Battle of Passchendaele, began on Oct.3rd. and after very heavy fighting Canadian troops reached the top of the Ridge and entered the rubble that was all that was

left of Passchendaele village on November 6th.1917. The final line was established by Nov.10th. and that is where it was held throughout the winter of 1917-18 for, although the Germans had been driven off the Ridges in 1917, they had not been beaten. The war was not yet over because the breakthrough that had been planned had not taken place. Indeed the Allies now had a larger Salient and a longer front line to defend, as they were to find to their cost in Spring 1918.

Third Battle of Ypres Jly. - Nov. 1917.

front line 30 Jly. 1917.
front line 31, Jly. 1917; (the battle of Pilckem Ridge).
front line 4, Oct. 1917; (the battle of Broodseinde).
front line 9, Oct. 1917; (the battle of Poelkapelle).
front line 10, Nov. 1917; (the battle of Passchendaele).

An easily missed artefact of war! One of the metal screw-pickets used to support barbed wire at the front 1914-18. It is now being used by a farmer for a similar purpose, but to keep his cows in the field, near the rebuilt village of Passchendaele.

THE BATTLE OF THE LYS(FOURTH YPRES),1918: in March 1918 the Germans launched several attacks along the Western Front in an all-out attempt to win the war. It became known as the Spring Offensive. On April 9th. one of these attacks was directed across the plain of the River Lys just to the south of Ypres - and it looked like being a success for the Germans. The very difficult decision was then made to withdraw the line around Ypres to make a much smaller, and thus more easily defendable, salient. All the gains of Messines and Third Ypres were given up, but now it was the German's turn to exhaust themselves in the mud in 1918. They could not withstand the Allied counter-attack of Sep. and Oct., war ending in Nov.

Battle of the Lys ('Fourth Ypres) Apr. 1918

front line 20 Mar. '18.
front line 29 Apr. '18.

CEMETERIES: early in the war it was decided that the recording and burial of the dead should be done as thoroughly as possible. This was far from easy. The dead were not removed from the battlefield and taken to their home countries, they were generally buried where they fell or died of wounds. A makeshift wooden cross would be set up with their name and number on it. Subsequent shelling often destroyed graves and many men were never formally buried due to the appalling conditions of war. However, every effort was made to establish cemeteries. This was helped by the French and Belgian Governments giving the British Empire 'in perpetuity' any land on which cemeteries were established, with the British being responsible for their maintenance. In May 1917 the Imperial War Graves Commission was set up to do this work, (being renamed the Commonwealth War Graves Commission in 1960).

The entrance gate to Tyne Cot Cemetery near Passchendaele.

They are also responsible for memorials such as the Menin Gate and the Memorial to the Missing at Tyne Cot which record the names of those with no known graves.

The dozens of cemeteries around Ypres thus mark for ever the places where the fighting occurred. In a very sad way they help us 'map out' the front lines of 1914-18. The dates on the headstones can also help us follow the progress of the battles around Ypres, individual cemeteries or parts of them being the unfortunate outcome of particular events.

The Commonwealth Cemeteries are peaceful and beautiful places. The rows of white Portland stone headstones are uniform in size and design, and carry, where it is known, the name, number, age, rank of the soldier and the date of his death. The badge of his service is included and the appropriate religious symbol. There is often an inscription at the base which relatives have chosen. Each cemetery has a name, a gateway, a Cross of Sacrifice, a Stone of Remembrance and a Register that lists the names of those buried there. The most impressive feature, however, is the garden-like feel of these places. The flowers and lawns are kept in immaculate condition. The aim to give the impression of an English country churchyard has indeed been achieved. The Commission employees work hard at home in England too; they will do their best to trace the graves of relatives if you wish to know where they are to be found.

Every cemetery has a Cross of Sacrifice, and the larger ones a Stone of Remembrance, designed by Sir Edwin L.Lutyens, inscribed with the words 'Their Name Livith for Evermore' from Ecclesiasticus which was suggested by Rudyard Kipling. He also chose the words 'Known Unto God' which is inscribed on the headstones of soldiers whose identity is unknown.

The Cemetery Register, found behind a metal door at the

entrances, are useful to us because they give information about the cemetery, the men there, such as their age and address, and a plan and reference scheme so that individual headstones can be located. Taking Essex Farm Cemetery, just north of Ypres, as an example (2 on map p12)the Register informs us that it was'named after a farm building occupying the narrow space between the road and the canal bank. The land south of the farm came into use as a Dressing Station Cemetery in April 1915, and it remained in use until August 1917'. It further informs us that 1088 British soldiers are buried there (of whom 102 are unknown), 9 Canadians, 83 whose unit is unknown, and 5 German prisoners (the occasional German headstones in British cemeteries are square-topped).

The Register sometimes gives more detail of particular men, e.g.Private T.Barratt V.C. at Essex Farm. He won the Victoria Cross in 1917, and the emblem is carved on his headstone. The Register gives the extract from the London Gazette of Sept.4th.1917 which describes the actions for which he won the medal: 'For conspicuous bravery when as Scout to a patrol he worked his way towards the enemy line with the greatest gallantry and determination, in spite of continuous fire from hostile snipers at close range. These snipers he stalked and killed'. Several similar actions are then described, the extract concluding: 'After safely regaining our lines this very gallant soldier was killed by a shell'.

Some of the cemeteries, memorials, etc. frequently visited are shown on the map on p12. These range from the largest Commonwealth War Cemetery Tyne Cot (No. 9 on map p12) containing 11,908 graves and a Memorial to the Missing where the 34,888 listed as missing after Aug.16th.1917 are named, to the very small cemeteries such as Woods and Hedgerow (No.15) and those in Ploegsteert Wood (No.21). A book which gives details of the cemeteries, memorials, and main features around Ypres, and along the whole Western Front, is 'Before Endeavours Fade' by Rose E.B.Coombs. This book, by an eminent authority on First World War battlefields, is an invaluable aid for visitors to Ypres and other Western Front areas today.

The German Military Cemetery at Langemarck: 10,143 Germans lie under the slabs beneath the oak trees of the rather sombre first section in this cemetery. A mass grave, also in this section, contains 24,834 men. As well as a further 9,500 men, the other section contains part of the German concrete fortifications with blocks carrying the names of the German fighting units whose members lie in the cemetery. The entrance building has a 'Student Room' where the names of the German student troops who died in the attack on Langemarck in Oct.1914 are carved. Another room contains a Register and a wood map of the Western Front.

Langemarck was fiercely fought over in 1914 but remained in Allied hands until the gas attacks of April 1915 when it fell to the Germans. It was recaptured in August 1917 in one of the early battles of 'Third Ypres', but was given up to the Germans again in the Allied withdrawal in the Spring of 1918. What little was left of the village was finally re-taken by the Allies in Sept.1918.The village has since been reconstructed.

SANCTUARY WOOD TRENCH MUSEUM (No.11 on map p12):

a portion of front line and support trenches dating from 1916 have been preserved here. An underground passageway of similar date can also be seen - and explored with a torch and boots!. Such artefacts help us to begin to understand what life was like for front-line troops in 1914-18. There is nearly always mud and water in the bottom of the trenches and the small sleeping dug-outs in the sides of the trench remind us that no one went home at the end of the day - the front-line had to be occupied at all times and in all weathers. Some of the 'trees' that were left standing in 1918 can still be seen, full of bullet holes and shell fragments. If, in your mind, you take the new trees and the grass away, it is easy to imagine the scene in 1914-18. The photograph of near-by Chateau Wood (just on the northern side of the Menin Road from Sanctuary Wood) taken in 1917 gives a good idea of what Sanctuary Wood must have been like.

In Oct.1914 the wood was complete and in a quiet area. It thus became the gathering point for Allied soldiers cut off from their units. While there they were protected from being given other duties without specific permission, hence it became known as 'Sanctuary Wood' - a 'safe' place. By 1915, however, it was less quiet as it became part of the front - line. In the summer of 1916 the Germans launched a number of attacks in the area, but were eventually driven back by the Canadians who retook Hill 62 which is close to the site of the Trench Museum. Indeed, the road leading up to the Museum is called Canadalaan (or Maple Avenue due to the lining of these trees that are Canada's emblem) because it leads to the Hill 62 Canadian Memorial commemorating their actions there in 1916.

The indoors part of Sanctuary Wood Museum has artefacts and photographs which also help us to understand what the front-line battle area was like in 1914-18. There are war-time pictures of Hill 62 and Sanctuary Wood, and also of the area around Passchendaele in 1917 - all scenes of total destruction. There are some stereoscopic photos. in the Museum which vividly reveal the horrors of war on the Western Front.

Some of the preserved trenches in Sanctuary Wood. This 'anti-blast' zig-zag plan was a common feature of trench construction.

The remains of one of the original trees of Sanctuary Wood - just about standing!.

Chateau Wood, Oct.29th. 1917, situated just to the north of Sanctuary Wood. (IWM E1220)

CROONART WOOD TRENCH MUSEUM (No.20 on map p12): opposite, one of the German concrete bunkers preserved in the wood; below, a 'wall' of shells near the Museum building. (photo: Bill Caudwell)

The trench lines and concrete bunkers preserved in CROONART WOOD are part of the German front-line of 1915-17 prior to the Battle of Messines. It is believed that Adolf Hitler, then a corporal in the German army, was wounded here in 1917. The owner of the Museum, André Becquart, has photographs of Hitler returning to view the spot in 1940 when war once again overtook this area.

A notable feature in the Museum grounds is the preserved German mine shaft. It is in excess of 30 metres deep and to peer down into the darkness helps us to understand what underground warfare on the Messines Ridge must have been like – for the British and Germans alike. The thought of descending this shaft and then tunnelling beneath enemy (in this case British) positions is not a pleasant one. The pond at the entrance to the museum is one of the outcomes of this tunnelling by the Germans, being a medium-sized mine crater (called 'Karl') where several Allied soldiers were killed when it was blown. The indoor section of the Museum has weapons, ammunition and many other artefacts.

Another War Museum well worth a visit is the extremely well laid-out collection of artefacts housed in part of the Town Hall in MESSINES. Someone is always on hand to answer visitor's questions. The actions of the New Zealand soldiers, who retook Messines in June 1917, are particularly commemorated.

WARNING!: Not all of the artefacts of war, such as shells and grenades, are safely contained in museums. Nor are they all 'dead'!. The two shells shown in the photograph opposite still have their fuse caps in place which means that they are 'live'!. Farmers place such objects by the roadside for the Belgian bomb disposal unit, based in Houthulst Forest (5 on map p12), that collects and deals with this 'harvest of death'. Contrary to what you might expect, explosives become more unstable and more dangerous the older they get. So, DO NOT TOUCH SUCH OBJECTS should you happen to see any in fields or by the roadside!. BE WARNED!!.

THE SECOND HALF OF THIS BOOKLET describes the battles around Ypres in more detail and mentions sites that can be visited today related to each battle. Further examples of ways of finding out about the past are also presented (see pages 22/23 and 31/32). Two points should be made now, however. First, it was mainly after the war that the historians labelled the actions around Ypres as the 'First Battle of Ypres', 'Second Ypres', etc. as they were the main 'set-piece' battles with recognisable beginnings and ends. Many men fought, and died in great numbers , in the Ypres Salient during the so-called 'quiet times' of just holding the line. Second, most places in the Ypres Salient were fought over several times between 1914 and 1918 and so, although some of the cemeteries, memorials, etc. relate mainly to one event, most span the events of the whole four years. Finally, a reminder that the Allies defended or attacked looking eastwards, while the Germans were attempting to move westwards to take Ypres and then capture the Channel ports, thus threatening Britain itself.

THE FIRST BATTLE OF YPRES, 1914: during Sept. and early Oct.1914 the Germans quickly spread their forces northwards towards the North Sea coast to avoid the British Expeditionary Force (BEF) and the French attacking the northern side (right flank) of their original 'spearhead' thrust towards Paris. The Allies moved north too in an attempt to do just what the Germans feared, i.e. outflank them. These moves became known as 'the race to the sea', which neither side 'won'. Instead they both ended up facing each other in a parallel set of trenches from the coast near Nieuport to south of the Ypres area, and indeed along the whole of what was called the Western Front south to Switzerland (see p11). The wet, muddy stalemate of almost static trench war-fare had begun, and was to continue for the next four years.

This slowing down of events did at least give the British a chance to bring more troops over to France to help out the pitifully small numbers of the BEF. In an effort to prevent this the Germans launched an attack in the northern part of the Western Front, especially around Ypres, aimed at taking Ypres and then marching quickly on to capture the Channel ports of Calais and Boulogne, thus preventing more British and her Empire troops coming to join the battle against them. The defence of Ypres thus became of vital importance. The first of the several 'rounds' in this bloody contest took place in Oct./Nov. 1914 and came to be known as the 'First Battle of Ypres'.

The Germans attacked Ypres from three sides, with fresh troops and in vastly superior numbers. Their partially encircling attack, from the north, south and east of the town, helped to create the 'bulge' in the Western Front around Ypres that was to remain as the 'Ypres Salient' until 1918 (see p11). The Germans suffered heavily in

The 1914 Household Brigade Memorial at Zandvoorde (10 on map p12). The Household Brigade, the aristocratic cavalry unit used to guarding royalty, took a gallant part in the defence of the Zand-voorde/Gheluvelt area in late Oct.1914. The Memorial stands on the spot where one of their officers, Lord Worsley, was killed on Oct.30th. 1914. This Memorial reminds us that the best of the British Regular Army, in terms of men and whole battalions, was lost in 'First Ypres' in 1914.

First Battle of Ypres 1914

— front line 22.Oct.'14
--- front line 22.Nov.'14

the northern sector around Langemarck in October when many of the Student Soldiers died (see p16). The line of the Salient was thus held in this area, indeed some gains were made by the Allies between Poelkapelle and Zonnebeke (see map opposite). In early November, however, Messines, Wytschaete (called 'Whitesheet' by the soldiers) and the Ridge on which they stood in the southern sector of the Salient fell to the Germans. This was a strategically important position (the few metres of height giving them an excellent view right across the Salient) which the Germans were not to lose until the Battle of Messines in June 1917 (see p25/26).

Fierce fighting took place in the central sector of the Salient along the Menin Road, especially at Gheluvelt (Geluveld). Early on Oct.31st.1914 the British line broke at this village and it looked as if Ypres was lost, and with it the Channel ports. Whole battalions were wiped out and others were cut off as the Germans moved through the gap. Then, in the early afternoon the 2nd.Worcesters charged the village and, by attacking the German's right flank (side), retook the village by 2.30 p.m. They had closed the gap and saved Ypres. They also rescued the survivors of the South Wales Borderers who had become cut off in the grounds of Gheluvelt Chateau. The Chateau is worth seeing to-day, though it is a reconsruction, the original not surviving the war, and there is a Memorial to the South Wales Borderers next to the derelict windmill in the village.

On Nov.11th. the Germans brought in their best troops, the Prussian Guard, to take Gheluvelt. They did not succeed in doing so, to the eternal credit of the British fighting man, but eventually, by sheer force of superior numbers, the village at the 'point' of the Salient did fall and the Allies were pushed back along the Menin Road towards Hooge and to the Zillebeke area (see map opposite). The battle ceased with the onset of bad weather in late November - and Ypres had been held!. But during those four weeks of stupendous struggles, and displays of immense bravery on both sides, the cream of both the Allied and German Regular Armies had been lost. The cemeteries and memorials relating to this time reflect this clearly (see those featured on this and the opposite page). Many of the old ideas died with the men who held them in 1914. Cavalry charges were replaced by trenches and machine guns. A different sort of war than any previously experienced lay ahead for the survivors of 1914 and their volunteer comrades (anxious to get to the war before it was over by Christmas!) to come.

The grave of an aristocratic officer of a crack Guards division in a plot within the Churchyard at Zillebeke (13 on map p12). The British had been pushed back to Zillebeke by mid Nov.1914. This early casualty of the war further signifies the loss of our Regular Army in 'First Ypres'.

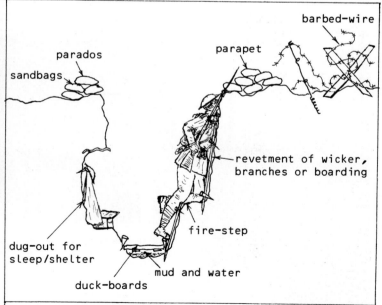

Cross-section of a trench. Such warfare was new to most soldiers in 1914, but they came to know it - too well!.

DURING THE WINTER OF 1914/15 it was discovered that winter warfare was very difficult in Flanders. Mud was the common enemy; conditions in the trenches were bad enough to cause as many casualties as gunfire. On Christmas Day 1914 near to Ploegsteert Wood ('Plugstreet' to the soldiers, see 21 on map p12) a spontaneous truce took place and the men who were officially enemies came out of their trenches, talked, and exchanged gifts in that desolated area between the opposing trenches called 'no man's land'. Such a thing was never to happen again, however, as old ideas and values continued to die as they had done during 'First Ypres'. But at least that battle had given each side a respect for the other's bravery and fighting ability. The spring of 1915, however, brought an event that was to severely embitter the Allied soldiers against the Germans.

SECOND YPRES, 1915: the Germans were as determined as ever to break through to the Channel ports in the spring of 1915. The Belgians had bravely flooded the area between Ypres and the coast in 1914, and the Germans had pushed as far as possible in the south of the Salient, so the thrust came in the northern sector. In the early evening of Apr.22nd.1915 the Germans used a secret weapon against French and French Colonial (Algerian) troops in the Steenstraat-Langemarck-Boezinge area to help them get the breakthrough they so desperately sought. The Canadian troops holding the line to the right of the French saw a yellowish cloud drifting on the wind south-westwards towards the French soldiers. It was poison gas (chlorine), and such a thing had never been used as a weapon of war before on the Western Front. The French troops were totally unprepared and ran back towards Ypres many of them blinded and all coughing violently. The frothy mucus which this gas creates in the lungs led to a prolonged and agonizing death.

The Memorial to the French 87th.and 45th.divisions that were involved in the gas attack on Apr.22nd. 1915. It is at Rose Crossroads about 1½ km east of Boezinge, as the sign indicates, in the Pilckem – Langemarck direction. The Memorial is in the form of two symbols of Brittany, the dolmen and the calvary. There is also a metal map which shows the area involved in the gas attack. (see 3 on map p12).

The Canadian Memorial at St.Julien, commemorating the gallant holding action they made against the gas attacks and heavy German bombardments between the 22nd. and the 24th. Apr. 1915.

The outcome of the German gas attack, and the tremendous artillery bombardment that accompanied it, was that a 6-7 km gap was opened up in the front line and Germans started to pour through towards Ypres. Apr.22nd.1915 looked as if it was going to be as critical a day as Oct.31st.1914. As then, deeds of immense heroism saved the day. Although the Allies used gas themselves later in the war, the defence of Ypres in Apr.1915 was partly inspired by the bitterness that was felt against the Germans for being the first to use such a 'cowardly' device in war.

It fell to the Canadians to seal up the gap in the line on the night of the 22nd., though they were eventually reinforced by a variety of British units rushed onto the scene. The Canadians extended their line westwards but were forced to fall back to St.Julien by the 23rd. (see map opposite). On the 24th it was the Canadian's turn to be attacked directly by gas. They resisted gallantly, but were forced to retire and give St.Julien up to the Germans.

The Second Battle of Ypres continued on into May and resulted in the Germans gaining all of the Passchendaele Ridge and the several smaller ridges lying between Ypres and Passchendaele in the northern sector of the Salient. The pressure had been put on from Hill 60 in the south (see p27) to Boezinge in the north and, as a result, by May 1915 the Germans had taken most of the Salient and Ypres was threatened by a front line only a few kilometres from her walls (see map opposite). In Dec.1915 the Germans launched a large-scale phosgene gas attack and bombardment, again in the northern sector of the Salient, in one last bid to break through to the Channel ports. But by now the Allied soldiers were equiped with protective gas masks; an unknown horror of a few months before was now a gruesome common-place!.

Though the Germans had failed to break through at Ypres in 1915, they started work straight away to take advantage of possessing the majority of the Salient area. During 1916 and into 1917, the Germans set about fortifying the areas they had won, especially the minor folds of land and, of course, the major Ridges, i.e. Passchendaele Ridge in the north and the Messines Ridge in the south. They built concrete pill boxes and deep dug-outs and bunkers. These almost impregnable bastions awaited the Allies when they attacked the Germans in 1917 and contributed to the bloodbath that was 'Third Ypres'.

The grave of Valentine Joe STRUDWICK in Essex Farm Cemetery (2 on map p12). He was killed on Jan.14th. 1916 aged 15, one of the youngest to die on the Western Front.

One way to find out about the past is to study one ordinary individual caught up in the events of history. Rifleman V.J.Strudwick died during a 'quiet' time in the Ypres Salient, a casualty of an 'in-between' time that historians gave no battle name to, but still a time when thousands died under the rain of shells that fell upon them as they held the line around Ypres. My pupils were always interested in Valentine because many were of the same age as he was when he died, his life ended at an age when they saw their's as stretching before them. I wanted to see if I could find out more about this lad who had obviously lied about his age in order to join the Army. Why had he done this, how did he get on at such a young age, and how had he died?. I thought I could find answers to these questions when, from the Cemetery Register, I found out that he came from Dorking, near my own home town.

The War Memorial in Dorking, Surrey, with V.J.Strudwick's name top left. Such Memorials record the dead of towns and villages who lie in foreign cemeteries where they fell.

I visited the Memorial in Dorking which includes Valentine's name. As my researches had started in the cemetery near Ypres where he lies, I knew from the Register there where he came from. It would be possible, if you wished to do so, to research a man named on a Memorial near your home even if you were unable to visit battlefields abroad first.

After leaving the Memorial in Dorking I visited the offices of the local newspaper, the 'Dorking Advertiser'. They hold back copies of the then 'Dorking & Leatherhead Advertiser'. As I knew the date of Valentine's death I was able to ask for the January 1916 issues. Local libraries sometimes have back issues of local papers and the British Museum Newspaper Library (address on back cover) holds complete runs of all newspapers. The article on Valentine Strudwick was very informative as you can see

"A GOOD SOLDIER."

Another Dorking lad has achieved honour by laying down his life for his country. Pte. Valentine Joe Strudwick, of the 8th Rifle Brigade, joined up twelve months ago last January, and at the time of his death, on Jan. 14th, he had not reached his sixteenth birthday, he having been born on St. Valentine's Day, 1900. His mother would naturally have liked to have kept him out of the Army for at least a year or two, but young Strudwick would not have it—a fine example to those of maturer years who have not yet joined, and perhaps a reproach! With only six weeks' training the lad was sent over to France. Within a short time he lost two of his chums who were standing near him—both instantaneously killed. The shock was such, with the addition of being badly gassed, that he was sent home and was for three months in hospital at Sheerness. On recovering he rejoined his regiment in France, and this week his mother received the following letter from his commanding officer, dated Jan. 15th: "I am very sorry indeed to have to inform you that your son was killed by a shell on Jan. 14th. His death was quite instantaneous and painless and his body was carried by his comrades to a little cemetery behind the lines, where it was reverently buried this morning. A cross is being made and will shortly be erected on his grave. Rifleman Strudwick had earned the goodwill and respect of his comrades and of his officers, and we are very sorry indeed to lose so good a soldier. On their behalf as well as my own I offer you our sincere sympathy." The deceased was Mrs. Strudwick's second surviving son, and her grief is the greater because of the fact that she had not been able to see him since he joined the Army. She has another son in the Royal Field Artillery. Young Strudwick was an old St. Paul's boy.

for yourself. If you have started with a name from a Memorial you will need to know the date he died to make best use of newspapers. Alternatively, you could start with the papers and look for an article on a man that catches your imagination. Then look for his name on the Memorial.

I then looked up 'Strudwick' in the telephone directory. Of those listed, one lived in the same street in Dorking given as Valentine's address in the Cemetery Register at Essex Farm. Relatives of Valentine told me more about him, but because he never returned home after joining the Army there is no photograph of him in uniform. Following a not very industrious time in school his jobs were bagging up coal and then helping on a smallholding He was a tall strong lad for his age. The Rifle Brigade records at Winchester show that he dropped his first name and just called himself Joe when he went away to Lambeth to join up. This, with his height, helped him to lie about his true age at the recruiting centre. His mother never saw him again. In running away to the Army in Jan.1915 Valentine Strudwick exchanged a very ordinary life for a place in history by becoming one of the youngest serving soldiers at the age of 14 years, 11 months. He died, at 15, 'a good soldier'.

This kind of research is quite possible whether you are also able to visit foreign battlefields or not. You may need an adult to assist you, however, when handling original documentary evidence or contacting relatives of the person you are studying.

The article on Valentine Strudwick and his death in the Jan.22nd.1916 'Dorking and Leatherhead Advertiser' -documentary evidence that helped answer questions about him. (Argus Newspapers)

IN FLANDERS FIELDS: It was at Essex Farm that John McCrae, a Canadian Medical Officer, wrote the now famous poem 'In Flanders fields'. The concrete dug-outs, seen beyond the cemetery opposite, and in close up below, were a Field Dressing Station dug into the canal bank. Some of the names pencilled on the interior walls date from the war, but most are of visiting relatives touring the battlefields in the 1920s and 30s. The dug-outs extended along the canal bank behind the cemetery itself, and it was here that Lt.Col.McCrae worked to save soldier's lives during the Second Battle of Ypres in 1915. Between the arrival of batches of wounded men John McCrae wrote his poem on a page torn from a dispatch book. The cemetery at Essex Farm is a sad indication that he was unable to save all of those he treated.

The canal at Essex Farm was close to the front line in 1915 (see map p21), and John McCrae was kept very busy. It is said that men who were shot in the trenches on top of the canal bank rolled down into his Dressing Station at its foot. McCrae died of pneumonia in 1918 and is buried in the British Communal Cemetery at Wimereux near Boulogne. Poppies like broken ground, and there was plenty of that on the battlefields of Ypres. McCrae's poem later inspired the use of the Flanders poppy as a symbol of remembrance for those who died in the war:

> In Flanders fields the poppies blow
> Between the crosses, row on row,
> That mark our place; and in the sky
> The larks still bravely singing fly
> Scarce heard amid the guns below.
>
> We are the dead. Short days ago
> We lived, felt dawn, saw sunset glow,
> Loved and were loved, and now we lie
>   In Flanders fields.
>
> Take up our quarrel with the foe;
> To you from failing hands we throw
> The torch; be yours to hold it high.
> If ye break faith with us who die
> We shall not sleep, though poppies grow
>   In Flanders fields.
>   John McCrae, 1915

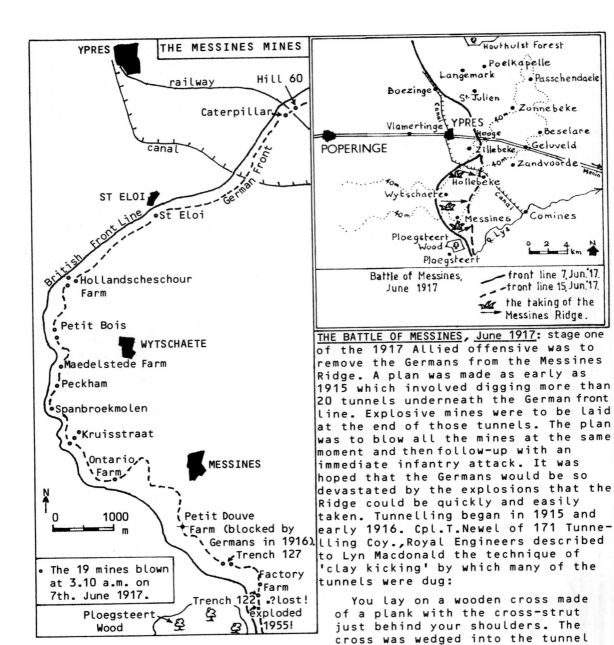

THE MESSINES MINES

YPRES

railway

Hill 60

Caterpillar

canal

German Front

British Front Line

ST ELOI

St Eloi

Hollandscheschour Farm

Petit Bois

WYTSCHAETE

Maedelstede Farm

Peckham

Spanbroekmolen

Kruisstraat

Ontario Farm

MESSINES

N

0   1000
         m

Petit Douve Farm (blocked by Germans in 1916)

Trench 127

Factory Farm

• The 19 mines blown at 3.10 a.m. on 7th. June 1917.

Trench 122 .?lost! exploded 1955!

Ploegsteert Wood

Houthulst Forest

Poelkapelle

Langemark

Passchendaele

Boezinge

St Julien

Zonnebeke

Vlamertinge

YPRES

Hooge

Beselare

POPERINGE

Zillebeke

Geluveld

Zandvoorde

Menin

Hollebeke

Wytschaete

canal

Messines

Comines

R. Lys

Ploegsteert Wood

Ploegsteert

0 2 4 km   N

Battle of Messines, June 1917

— front line 7. Jun. '17.
-- front line 15. Jun. '17.

the taking of the Messines Ridge.

THE BATTLE OF MESSINES, June 1917:

stage one of the 1917 Allied offensive was to remove the Germans from the Messines Ridge. A plan was made as early as 1915 which involved digging more than 20 tunnels underneath the German front line. Explosive mines were to be laid at the end of those tunnels. The plan was to blow all the mines at the same moment and then follow-up with an immediate infantry attack. It was hoped that the Germans would be so devastated by the explosions that the Ridge could be quickly and easily taken. Tunnelling began in 1915 and early 1916. Cpl.T.Newel of 171 Tunnelling Coy., Royal Engineers described to Lyn Macdonald the technique of 'clay kicking' by which many of the tunnels were dug:

You lay on a wooden cross made of a plank with the cross-strut just behind your shoulders. The cross was wedged into the tunnel so that you were lying at an angle of forty-five degrees with your feet towards the face. You worked with a sharp-pointed spade with a foot-rest on either side above the blade, and you drove the blade into the clay, kicked the clay out, and on to another section, moving forward all the time.

Several times the Germans had almost discovered the tunnels by the use of listening devices and counter-tunnelling. It was mainly that the tunnels were at a greater depth than the Germans expected which prevented their discovery, though one was discovered and blocked by them in 1916 at Petit Douve Farm (see map above).

Spanbroekmolen (or Lone Tree) Mine Crater is now owned by Toc H and called the 'Pool of Peace'. This, the largest of the 1917 mine craters, is an excellent example of how the evidence of that remarkable June day is preserved for us to see today. Several of the other nineteen craters are also still to be seen.

By early 1917 nearly all the tunnels had been finished and the mines laid. The explosion of the mines was planned for precisely 3.10a.m. on June 7th.1917. Captain M.Greener of 175 Tunnelling Coy.,Royal Engineers was facing the spot where the Spanbroekmolen mine was about to be blown. Then all the mines were blown. Some described it as being like an earthquake. It is said that the noise of the explosions was heard in London. Captain Greener describes what he saw:

> The earth seemed to open and rise up to the sky. It was all shot with flame. The dust and smoke was terrific. And all this debris falling back.

The explosions had the desired effect as Rifleman T.Cantlon,21st. King's Royal Rifles explained to Lyn Macdonald:

> They (the Germans) didn't seem to have any wits about them.... We just saw them coming at us through the smoke, running towards us like jellies. They didn't know where they were.

Under these circumstances the infantry attack which immediately followed the explosions was very successful and the Messines Ridge was taken from the Germans in a matter of hours.

One tragedy occurred at Spanbroekmolon, however. Some Irish troops went

forward seconds _before_ the mine exploded and were caught in the falling debris. Ltn.T.Witherow,8th.Btn.Royal Irish Rifles recalls that:

> ...We were all thrown violently to the ground and debris began to rain down on us. Luckily only soft earth fell on me,.. but the Lance Corporal ...was killed by a brick.

Spanbroekmolen Cemetery (about 200m from the crater;Lone Tree Cemetery is also near-by). All the dead are Irish and all died on June 7th.1917. The crater and the two cemeteries near it help us piece together the events of that June morning over sixty years ago.

HILL 60: was where the most northerly of the mines was exploded on June 7th. 1917 as the opening move in the Battle of Messines. Another mine was exploded at the same time, the Caterpillar mine, just on the other side of the railway cutting from Hill 60. Infact, Hill 60, so named in 1914 because it was 60 metres high, was a man-made hill, being the earth taken from the cutting when the railway was built many years before.

So, Hill 60 was little more than a pile of earth, but it was strategic--ally very important indeed. When the Germans captured the hill on Dec. 10th. 1914 they not only looked down on the British front-line a few metres away, but they also commanded a clear view of Ypres beyond. If you stand on Hill 60 today and look towards Ypres (a mere 3½km. away) you can put yourself in their place and see what an excellent advantage these few metres of height provided.

An attempt was made in 1915 to remove the Germans from the hill by tunnelling and mining. On the evening of April 17th. 1915 five small-to-medium mines were blown. Some of the craters can still be seen today just to the left of the entrance to Hill 60. After several days of bitter fighting the British took the hill, but early in May the Germans won it back again, mainly through the use of poisonous gas attacks. They remained on the hill, fortifying it with reinforced concrete 'pillboxes', until that fateful June morning in 1917 when the big mine was blown.

Tunnelling for the 1917 mine began in August 1915 at Hill 60. As the map below shows, a main tunnel was dug with two branches at the end, one to Hill 60, the other under the Caterpillar. The Hill 60 mine was in place by July 1916 and the Caterpillar by October. Fierce fighting above

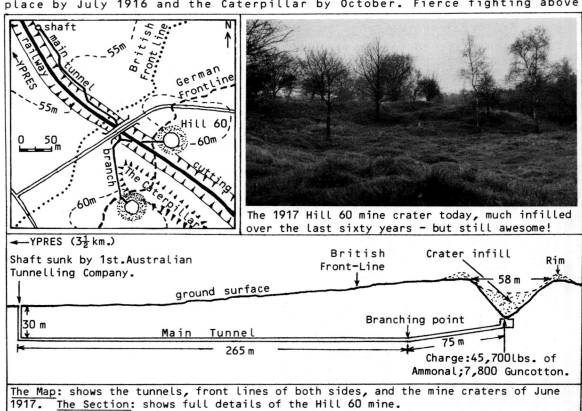

The 1917 Hill 60 mine crater today, much infilled over the last sixty years - but still awesome!

The Map: shows the tunnels, front lines of both sides, and the mine craters of June 1917. The Section: shows full details of the Hill 60 mine.

Hill 60, Aug.1917: the dreaded 'pile of earth' was now in British hands following the mining of June 1917. The hill was riddled with passages and dug-outs. A shattered German pillbox can be seen on top of the hill.   (IWM E 4604)

and below ground was needed to prevent the tunnels and mines being detected by the Germans while the detonation day in June 1917 was awaited. When the day did eventually come, Ltn.J.Todd,11th.Btn.Prince of Wales' Own Yorkshire Regiment described to Lyn Macdonald how it felt in those last tense moments. Had the Germans discovered the mine after all?:

It was an appalling moment. We all had the feeling,"It's not going!". And then a most remarkable thing happened. The ground on which I was lying started to go up and down just like an earthquake. It lasted for seconds and then, suddenly in front of us the Hill 60 mine went up.

Immediately after the explosion Todd and his comrades advanced on the hill. It was taken in a matter of minutes. He describes taking the German front line and then reaching the top of the hill:

...And, of course, we found a lot of German pillboxes up there and had to clear them out. There were quite a few Germans in them and we'd shout in to them to come out; if they didn't, then we chucked a bomb in. They came out fast enough then!.

Hill 60 was re-taken by the Germans following their Spring Offensive in April 1918. It was soon back in British hands, however, when the final Allied offensive pushed the Germans back in late September and early October 1918. The hill has been preserved as a memorial to the men who

fought and died on and beneath it. At the entrance an inscribed stone concludes:

In the broken tunnels beneath this enclosure many British and German dead were buried and the hill is therefore preserved so far as nature will permit in the state in which it was left after the Great War.

Hill 60 today: 'preserved so far as nature will permit'. The pillbox was originally German (see bottom right) but was added to by British troops after 1917 (see upper part).

28

THE THIRD BATTLE OF YPRES,1917: following the great success of Messines in June, the British Commander-in-Chief, Sir Douglas Haig, was keen to begin phase two of his plan to push the Germans out of the Ypres Salient. This involved attacking the northern sector, particularly the Passchendaele Ridge. This was a different proposition to Messines, however, because the landscape was different. There were a number of smaller ridges and also stream valleys to cross, and capture, before the main Passchendaele Ridge was even reached (see section below and map p 12). No surprise tactics like mines could be used, this would have to be an 'over the top and storm the enemy lines' approach. This had proved deadly in the Somme Battles of 1916 and the British Prime Minister, Lloyd-George, was afraid Third Ypres could be the same. A French Army mutiny, a planned link-up with a British naval attack on the German-held Belgian ports, and Haig's belief in various intelligence reports that the Germans would give way, eventually won qualified approval for the Flanders campaign to go ahead.

A frontal attack on an enemy in 1914-18 comprised rising from the cover of your trenches and walking, heavily laden with equipment, weapons, gas-mask, etc., towards the enemy trenches. Opposition rifle and machine-gun fire led to heavy casualties. To counter this, such attacks would be preceded by a massively heavy bombardment of shells aimed at pulverising the enemy in his trenches, so that when you advanced there was little opposition. There was also a 'creeping barrage' of shells fired while you advanced. Shells were aimed to drop just in front of you, and, as you moved forward the shells would be fired a little further, i.e. the barrage would 'creep forward' just ahead of you clearing away any opposition that had somehow survived the pre-attack heavy bombardment. It does seem reasonable and perfectly sound, in theory that is!. In practice, however, almost as soon as the Third Battle of Ypres got under way on the 31st. of July 1917 things began to go badly, and sadly, wrong.

Three main problems arose. First, it rained!. The summer and autumn of 1917 turned out to be particularly wet in Flanders. This is potentially disastrous in such a low-lying clay area. The second problem ensured that the Allies turned this potential disaster into a real one themselves, i.e. the pre-attack bombardments destroyed field drains and stream banks in the battle area. As a consequence the rain and drizzle that always seemed to fall just as a major Allied attack was launched had no means of running away. As the campaign progressed through August and into September the ground between Ypres and the Passchendaele Ridge turned into a quagmire of foot-deep mud and water-

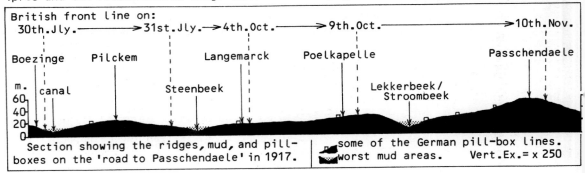

Third Battle of Ypres Jly. - Nov. 1917:
— front line 30 Jly. 1917.
— front line 31. Jly. 1917; (the battle of Pilckem Ridge).
--- front line 4. Oct. 1917; (the battle of Broodseinde).
-- front line 9. Oct. 1917; (the battle of Poelkapelle).
-·- front line 10. Nov. 1917; (the battle of Passchendaele).

British front line on:
30th.Jly. → 31st.Jly. → 4th.Oct. → 9th.Oct. → 10th.Nov.

Boezinge   Pilckem   Langemarck   Poelkapelle   Passchendaele

m. canal   Steenbeek   Lekkerbeek/
60   Stroombeek
40
20
0

Section showing the ridges, mud, and pill-boxes on the 'road to Passchendaele' in 1917.
some of the German pill-box lines. worst mud areas. Vert.Ex.= x 250

Thick glutinous mud!. An additional enemy not accounted for in the plans for 'Third Ypres'in the summer of 1917. The rain, and the barrage of shells laid down by guns like this, and large artillery pieces, turned the battle area into a quagmire. This gun became stuck during the first stage of the battle, at Pilckem Ridge, 2nd.August 1917.
(IWM Q5938)

filled shell-holes. The stream valleys became impassable 'mud-seas'. The third, and most devastating problem, was the amazing network of concrete strong-points which the Germans had built in the Salient areas they won in Second Ypres in 1915. The ridges and valleys bristled with them (see section opposite). They were of simple design;very thick reinforced concrete walls and roof (with a covering of turf to prevent detection from the air), a door at the back ('friendly side'), and slits to fire rifles and machine-guns from at the front ('enemy side')-see p31,33. Only the most accurate and direct hit from a heavy shell could destroy them. They were the German 'secret weapon' of Third Ypres because they effectively ruined the Allied attack strategy described on p29. The pre-attack bombardment did not pulverise the enemy because they were not in the open trenches they were in the concrete 'pill-boxes' and underground shelters. In fact, the Germans found that the end of a bombardment usually meant an attack was about to begin and were ready. So, when the Allied soldiers advanced, instead of meeting little opposition, they met pillboxes spitting deadly fire. And they got stuck in the

mud at the same time. It was living Hell!. As a consequence, the taking of each ridge, valley, and village on the way to Passchendaele turned into individual battles in their own right. Thus the Third Battle of Ypres became several battles (see map opposite), the final one, to take the Passchendaele Ridge itself, not beginning until early October 1917, over two months after the start of the campaign in July!.

A German 'pill-box' near Langemarck German Cemetery (see 4a on map p12), part of the 'Langemarck Line' of fortifications (also to be seen in the Cemetery, see p16) met by the Allies when they attacked the area in Sept./Oct.1917. The Memorial is to the 34th.Div.Royal Artillery who fought here in 1917. Once captured these pill-boxes were useful, providing the only shelter in the sea of mud. This box did so in Oct.1917.

FRANK BASTABLE, aged 86, served with the 7th.Battn. Royal West Kent Regt. 1914-19. He kindly spoke to me about his experiences during that time, an example of finding out about the past from the personal recollections of those who were there.

An interesting way of finding out about past events, especially ordinary people's experiences of them, is from the recollections of those who were there. Frank Bastable kindly gave me his memories of serving on the Somme in 1916 and at Ypres in 1917. I have also talked to veterans of the 1914-18 war at meetings of the 'Western Front Association', an organization aimed at furthering the understanding of events on the Western Front 1914-18 (NOT the glorification of war!), founded by John Giles in 1980 (address for details on back cover). We have already seen some examples in this booklet of how Lyn Macdonald took

spoken (oral) history as the basis for her work,(see p6, quotes from 'They Called It Passchendaele', and bibliography).

Frank Bastable volunteered for service in Sept.1914,"Because everyone was going from Chislehurst, I thought I might as well". Sent to France in July 1915, he fought on the Somme in 1916 where he was wounded for the first time. I asked him about Ypres, where he was sent in Oct.1917, to take part in the Third Battle of Ypres:

> There were these streams, or there had been, near where I was at Poelkapelle, but the shells had broken their banks. That's what made it so bad, there was mud everywhere. Me and the Sergeant pulled one bloke out, he was up to his neck in this shell-hole. We managed to get him out after a struggle, small north-country chap he was, but he didn't seem to be able to walk, I don't know why. So, we just laid him down, we had to get on. I still wonder now whether or not he was alright afterwards.

Private 1959 Bastable, F.H., just after he had voluntarilly joined the Army at Chislehurst, Kent in September 1914.

A line of German strong-points, known as 'pill-boxes' to the Allied troops, at Poelkapelle in 1917. The iron mesh that reinforced the concrete can be seen in the damaged pill-box nearest to the camera. The thickness of the walls and the reinforcing made these strong-points very difficult indeed to destroy. Arranged in lines, as seen in this picture, they were very difficult for foot soldiers to pass as, together, they had a complete field of fire in front of them. Tanks stood a better chance, and were used, but the mud made them immobile (see p33). It was when he came up against some of these pill-boxes at Poelkapelle (indeed possibly those in this picture), that Frank Bastable was wounded in October 1917 during the Third Battle of Ypres. Such lines of defences made any major advance very difficult indeed during Third Ypres, and helped account for the fact that it took the Allied soldiers from July to November to reach and take the Passchendaele Ridge, a distance of only about 9 km. (photo: Daniel, Ypres)

Frank Bastable in his hospital uniform at Sheffield where he was sent for treatment after being wounded near the village of Poelkapelle during Third Ypres in Oct.1917.

Frank also told me about the 'pill-boxes' at Poelkapalle, and being wounded there in Oct.1917:

We came up at night, it was raining, it was always raining!. There were quite good trenches at first, but the nearer the front line we came the worse it got. In the end it was just shell-holes and mud, always plenty of mud. They had these pill-boxes, concrete, nothing could knock them out. They had these slits they fired from. I came up against one and couldn't get on ... and I got stuck in the mud. The sergeant said that if I didn't get along quicker he'd shoot me!.

You don't know how you do dodge the shells and the bullets there were so many of them flying about. Well, I didn't, I got hit. The bullet went in the front of my leg and out through my back-side. I fell into a shell-hole. I knew I had to get back but it was a long way back to the Dressing Station, I must have walked miles. I don't know even now how I did it, but I made it in the end. I saw a bloke walking back with a piece of shell a foot long in his arm!. There were two German prisoners at the Dressing Station -they weren't bad blokes, you know, they had to do it the same as us- they made sure that the orderly saw to me first, before them. I was shipped home to hospital in Sheffield. I was pretty bad for a time, I wasn't well when that photo. was taken.(See above.)

Frank talked to me of other things, like receiving ten days First Field Punishment in 1916, when on the Somme, because his rifle went off while he was on parade. This meant being tied to the wheel of a wagon for two hours a day!. He also showed me a picture of the chapel at Talbot House in Poperinge near Ypres, where he was confirmed in 1917. Talbot House, abbreviated to 'Toc H', was a rest centre for men of all ranks founded by Col.Reginald Talbot and named in memory of his brother, Lt.Gilbert Talbot, who is buried in Sanctuary Wood Cemetery.

It has only been possible to present a few snippets of Frank Bastable's memories here, but they should help fulfil my aim of introducing you to this method of finding out about the past. It can be used for topics other than war-time recollections, but obviously must concern times and events with surviving witnesses. Twentieth century topics clearly have potential for including oral history as a source of evidence. You should get an adult to help you with this approach, however, at least when making the first contacts with people. Always be polite and make it clear why you wish to talk to people about their past life, and what you intend to do with the information.

This photograph, taken in France in 1919, shows the ten survivors of the original 1100 strong 7th. Btn., Royal West Kents of 1914. Not all of the others were killed, however, some finishing the war attached to other units. However, many of that 1100 never returned to Kent. Frank Bastable (seen here back row, second left) was one of the lucky ones who came back.

Passchendaele Ridge, Oct.1917: the Allied soldiers advanced across this 'sea' of mud and water in the final stages of Third Ypres in Oct/Nov.1917; it became known as the 'Battle of Passchendaele'. The use of tanks to knock out pillboxes and generally clear the way for the foot soldiers was a failure because they sank into the mud or fell into the shell-holes.   (IWM CO2241)

THE BATTLE OF PASSCHENDAELE, Oct/Nov.1917: the final battle of Third Ypres was launched against the village of Passchendaele itself, the aim being to secure the Ridge before winter. Battles on Oct.4th. (see Tyne Cot below) and Oct.9th. had brought the Allies to the foot of the Ridge; the final assault was about to begin. Conditions on the Ridge were appalling, heavy rain and shelling having produced a total morass. The attack on Passchendaele was planned for Oct.30th. The Canadians were to go from the well named Waterfields and Marsh Bottom area, up the valley of the Sroombeek and the higher ground flanking it, and straight for Passchendaele. The Royal Naval Divisions and a London Territorial Division were to advance along the Bellevue Spur to the north of the valley, while the Australians were to move along a line from near Tyne Cot towards Passchendaele south of the Stroombeek valley (see map opposite).   Pte.J.Pickard MM, 78th.Btn.Winnipeg Grenadiers described the morning of Oct.30th.1917 to Lyn Macdonald:

> The bombardment was murderous -ours and the Germans'- and they weren't only flinging over shells, they were simply belting machine-gun fire for all they were worth. But it was a case of "Over the top with the best of luck".

He went on to describe the method of 'advance':

> ... the only way we could move was to dodge from one (shell) hole to another, hoping that lightning really didn't strike twice in the same place. ... I splashed and wallowed through the mud, hoping I was going in the right direction, but none too sure.

TYNE COT CEMETERY: is situated on the slopes of the Passchendaele Ridge. It was a Northumbrian Division that named the group of German pillboxes here 'Tyne Cot'. The 2nd. Australian Division captured these strongpoints on Oct.4th.1917. The graves of those who died in this attack are behind the Cross of Sacrifice, which has been built on top of one of the blockhouses they captured. Two of the captured pillboxes were used by the Canadians, one as a Field Dressing Station, the other a stretcher-bearer's base. These two pillboxes can be seen within the bounds of the Cemetery today. The one pictured here, to the right of the Cemetery entrance, was the Dressing Station where the doctors worked less than 1 km from the front line in 1917. The one used as a stretcher-bearer's base is to the left of the entrance. After the war, 11,500 dead were brought from the surrounding battlefields and buried here, hence the large number of neatly laid out graves we see today. The Memorial to the Missing, listing those who fell in the Ypres Salient Aug.16th.1917 to the end of the war but who have no known grave, is on the curved back wall of the Cemetery. There are 34,888 names.   (See also p16; 9 on the map p12)

Passchendaele   Crest Farm   Stroombeek

The approaches to Passchendaele village seen from the New British Cemetery on Bellevue Spur. The Canadians battled their way, from the right, up the valley of the Stroombeek and the higher ground flanking it (see foreground and distance), reaching Crest Farm on Oct.30th.1917, and entering the village itself, then just rubble, on Nov.10th.

Somehow, the Canadians made it up onto the crest of the Passchendaele Ridge before the end of that murderous day, Oct.30th.1917. Pte.Pickard remembers it well:

> It was a place they called Crest Farm. They had to fight hard to get it and the place was thick with bodies. But we took it, and we held the line.

On Bellevue Spur the Naval and Territorial Divisions got badly stuck in the mud, and the New British Cemetery there stands as a reminder of the heavy casualties they suffered at that time.

On Nov.6th. the Canadians made the final push into the village of Passchendaele, not that there was much of a village left following all the bombardments. The Battle of Passchendaele, and with it Third Ypres, ended on Nov.10th.1917 when the final line was established for the winter. The Ridge had been won at great cost in terms of human lives lost. Some say half a million Allied and German soldiers died in the $3\frac{1}{2}$ month campaign of Third Ypres. Cpl.H.C.Baker 28th.Btn.Canadian Expeditionary Force vividly summed it up when he described his battalion's roll-call, following the battle, to Lyn Macdonald:

> .. If there was no response when a name was called, the sergeant would shout out, "Anybody know anything about him?". Sometimes someone replied. More often there was silence. My impression was that we had won the ridge and lost the battalion .....

As a result of the German Spring Offensive in 1918, all of the Allied gains of 1917, i.e. the Messines and Passchendaele Ridges, were to be given up to the Germans again!.

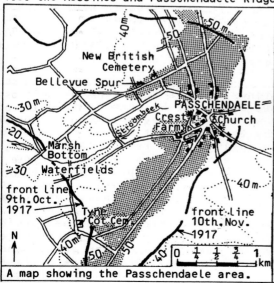

A map showing the Passchendaele area.

Crest Farm: now a Memorial commemorating the valiant Canadian's deeds here in Oct/Nov.1917. They struggled up this slope, through mud and against bullets on Oct.30th. A walk up this lane, from Waterfields to Passchendaele, helps one imagine the scene in 1917, with the men wallowing in the mud. The remains of many of those men still lie beneath the peaceful fields we pass as we walk up this gentle and pleasant slope today.

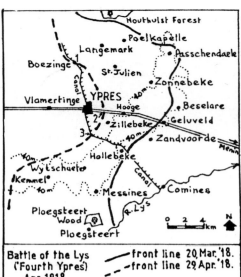

BATTLE OF THE LYS (Fourth Ypres),Apr.1918:
the spring of 1918 was a dark time for the
Allies. All of the ground gained in 1917
through the Battle of Messines and Third
Ypres was lost in just one month. Infact,
the Germans won ground they had never
before taken such as Kemmel. Ypres very
nearly fell. The Germans came so close tha
the town was defended from the actual wall
All this was the result of the German
'Spring Offensive' aimed at breaking
through the British and French lines in an
all-out attempt to win the war.

On March 20th. the German offensive was
launched against the Somme section of the
Western Front. They made great advances
and it was only by sheer determination tha
the Allies established and held a line.
The main attack was then concentrated in
the north across the plain of the R.Lys
just south of Ypres. The Germans intended
to rush past Ypres, take St.Omer and then

**Battle of the Lys
('Fourth Ypres)
Apr. 1918**
front line 20,Mar.'18.
front line 29.Apr.'18.

march on to the Channel ports and victory. The battle started on Apr.9th
1918. There were very heavy casualties on both sides and it looked as if
the Germans were going to take Ypres. At this point it was decided to
contract the Salient to a much smaller and thus more easily defended area
Passchendaele was given up to the Germans and soon Messines and Wytchaet
fell. A bitter blow indeed!. However, now it was the German's turn to
suffer in the Flanders mud where, on top of four long years of fighting,
they quickly exhausted themselves. So, the spring offensive of 1918
turned out to be the German army's last 'gasp' - but it had very nearly
succeeded!.

In September and October of 1918 an Allied counter offensive pushed the
Germans back for good, but not before the Menin Road and many other of
the dreadfully familiar places of the previous four years fighting had
been bloodily fought for all over again. The war ended with an armistice
or truce, being declared to come into effect on the eleventh hour of the

eleventh day of the eleventh month of 1918. So,
no one had 'won' outright. The Germans were wor
out just a little earlier than the Allies!. Abou
ten million people died in the process.

Demarcation Stones, such as the one shown here,
were set up all along the Western Front after
the war. They were put wherever roads or street
were crossed by the line that marked the maximu
German advance in 1918 - to remind us for ever
of how close the Germans had come to 'winning
through'. They bear the inscription 'Here the
Invader was brought to a standstill'. The ston
shown here, at Boezinge just north of Ypres, ha
the equipment and helmet of a French soldier
carved on it because the French held that secto
of the line. Other stones can be seen near Ypre
at Hellfire Corner (see 2 on the map above) and
by the canal (see 3 on map). These have British
helmets as British soldiers held this sector.